Toddler Discipline

---

5 Things You Must Know To Have A Well-Behaved Toddler In No Time!

Table of Contents

(This page has been intentionally left blank)

Why You Need To Read This Book

Does your toddler constantly push your buttons?

Do you feel like you're toddler makes you stressed, and you don't know how to give them discipline without feeling guilty?

Does your toddler have an attitude, throws tantrums, and often doesn't listen?

Do you hate the feeling when your toddler plays-up in public and people are watching how you handle it?

It's so frustrating right!

If you answer yes to any of these questions, then this book will help you discover how to have a well-behaved toddler in no time!

Even if you thought it is impossible.

In this book you'll discover:

- How and why they act the way they do (learning these principles will help you understand the world through their eyes)

- How to respond to your child without overreacting (it's much simpler than you think)

- The 3 best strategies for disciplining with positivity (this will reduce your stress too)

- The most common parents/caregivers make (and how to avoid them)

- How to be a positive role-model for your child (these tips will help create a strong bond between you both)

Chapter One: How Toddlers Act and Why?

The age between 2 and 3 is quite an exciting time for the toddler as well as the parents.

But even though toddlers at this age start learning language skills, they don't really understand logic and can have a difficult time exercising self-control.

How To Handle Their Strong Feelings

As a parent, you will have to help your toddler to control the strong emotions they experience especially during this age.

This isn't such a small task and may require quite a bit of patience and effort from your side.

Between the age of 2 and 3 toddlers often start to experience a stream of feelings such as guilt, shame, pride and embarrassment.

Your child is going to need a lot of love and guidance from you as a parent to cope with these changes.

You know your toddler is struggling when:

- They experience a meltdown when you are unable to understand their words.

- They get angry and might start throwing toys around

- They end up saying no when they actually mean yes

- They cannot work with a substitute. For instance, if you give them the green ball instead of the red, they might throw a fit and become inconsolable.

- They start acting out when they feel frustrated.

- On the other hand, after you have taught your child to manage his or her feelings, this is how they act:

  1. Starts using actions or words to ask for what they want.

  2. Tries to enact a stressful event, like a visit to the doctor.

  3. Starts expressing their anger and use words like "I am mad" instead of taking action on it.

4. Tries to impose the same rules on you as you imposed on them.

Five Facts You Should Know

1. All humans communicate through behavior. If your toddler is acting out, or angry, then you should know that there is something that they are trying to communicate. Children are always communicating something or other through their behavior. Inappropriate behavior is a signal that something isn't right and you need to get to the root cause of it.

2. There is always a reason behind the problematic behavior of your kid. If your kid always starts crying when you talk to someone else, then he or she is trying to get your attention. It's also a sign that he is gaining some kind of sensory pleasure out of it. But regardless, there is always a reason behind it.

3. As parents, we need to interpret our kid's challenging behavior. This can help us figure out the real meaning behind it. Children who display difficult behavior require a certain consistency of a loving and nurturing adult who

the child can rely on for guidance and support. Similarly, it's important that we learn to interpret the messages they are trying to convey through their actions.

4. There can be different reasons behind one specific behavior. For instance, if your child is angry, then the reason behind that could be anger, shame, guilt, or even hurt. Some children also engage in behaviors which seem destructive such as hitting their loved ones, throwing things, breaking things, etc. If this looks like your child, then you need to lend extra support to your kid to be able to first understand and then correct their behavior.

5. Focus on correcting your kid's behavior by using support and not punishment. When you punish your kid, he or she will feel disrespected and, as a result, start acting in ways, which are even more harmful. When you use harsh words or raise your hand against your kid, you are only teaching him how to suppress their behavior, rather than allowing them to correct it. When you start using positive ways to communicate with your toddlers, they will also

find positive ways to communicate with you, thereby allowing good behavior.

Chapter Two: How To Respond To Your Child Without Overreacting

Do you often end up reacting to your child's behavior instead of responding?

Reacting implies that you are matching your toddler's emotional charged reaction with your own intense reactions.

If your toddler starts throwing things at you, you start yelling at them.

If they are throwing a tantrum, you start working hard to quiet them down.

Now, let's see what responding looks like?

Responding, on the other hand, offers your child permission to start expressing their emotions, feelings, and ideas without feeling any type of guilt, shame and criticism.

If your toddler ends up becoming upset, you allow them to be so, instead of trying hard to control them.

You don't need to change your mind or be able to fix the issue.

This may not seem easy to you, especially if you have a busy schedule, and just can't seem to find enough patience to be mindful of your behavior towards your toddler.

But you should know that you are not alone and that a lot of parents struggle when it comes to this particular area.

Now, responding to situation can feel a little ineffective at the moment.

However, the payoff is great in the long run.

You are essentially teaching your child that it's safe to express their feelings, which will make them trust that you will be able to handle them when they are processing more intense emotions.

On the other hand, if you are someone who reacts, then it may take some time before responding comes more naturally to you.

The key is to have patience and some consistency.

If you happen to slip up, allow yourself permission to give it another try.

It is not regarded as a sign of weakness when you say something on the lines of, "Wait, this is what I meant to say..."

Let your toddler to know that you can make mistakes too.

Reacting Vs. Responding

Lets' look at a few examples which differentiate between reacting and responding.

- Stop it; will you Vs. is there something that upsets you? Do you want me to hug you?

- If you don't, stop yelling, I am going to take that toy away Vs. I am going to stop driving until you calm yourself down

- Oh god, you spilled milk on the carpet again? Vs. Oops, let me clean that mess for you.

- You are grounded Vs. I know you are upset, but I need to do this.

Now, let's look at some tips which will teach you how to avoid overreacting:

1. Take a few deep breaths whenever your toddler starts doing something that might urge you to react impulsively. Start counting to 10. Allow yourself to process what you are actually feeling. Are you sure you are angry with the child and not someone else? Are you angry with yourself? NO matter what your reason is, make sure that you don't raise a hand on your child.

2. Get away from the house at some point during the day and indulge in light-hearted activities like walking, running, and meeting up with other people, etc. Also, make it a habit to take your toddler along for a walk outside the house at least once a day.

3. Don't cut off social contact. In fact, try to connect with other parents while you are taking a stroll with your child. This allows for a healthy conversation to flow and brings a new perspective to your life.

4. Take short vacations whenever possible and travel to different destinations with your family. If this doesn't seem possible, you can

simply visit different places around the city to make life more fun for you as well as the toddler.

5. Make sure that you grab some down time while your toddler is sleeping. Indulge in as many relaxation activities as possible to avoid having a meltdown.

6. Arrange for a friend or a neighbor or relative to babysit your kid when you are tired. Remember, you don't have to get it done all by yourself. A little help along the way also strengthens the bond between people.

7. Lastly, do not judge or keep ruminating about the situation your toddler puts you into. You should not just be able to control your temper, but also forget if he or she does something that upsets you.

Chapter Three: Three Strategies To Discipline Your Toddler

My son wailed out of frustration, but each time I volunteered to help him, he kept screaming that he wanted to do it all by himself.

His reactions started getting intense, to the point that they plummeted towards me like a hurricane.

Over the last few months, I have started to get a grip on the "angry mom" inside me.

At the same time, I have learned how to discipline my child in such a way that it leaves a positive impact on him.

If you find it difficult to deal with a toddler who is too strong-willed or someone who has a tendency to cross his or her boundaries very often, then these 3 strategies will help you cope up with it.

Give Information

When your toddler is acting out, you should understand that he or she is trying their best to deal with the situation.

They just don't know any better than the way they are behaving.

So, it becomes your responsibility to give them information.

This is not about teaching or fixing them, you are just going to give them clear information, and so they can decide for themselves how they chose to react.

- When you give more information about a situation, this is what it might look like.

- You are not pulling the pants up the way you want to.

- You should ask for my help.

- You are angry that you can't put your pajamas on.

The point of giving information to your toddler is to let him know that you understand his or her side of the story.

Your toddler won't listen until you take this step.

Once he or she starts feeling heard or understood by you, it's only then that you can expect them to allow your guidance.

Avoid Letting Boundary Testing Ruffle You

I get it. When your kid starts throwing clothes, food or even toys onto the floor it's not easy to get a grip on your anger.

It is going to take a lot of self-control for you to be able to stay calm.

If your child refuses to listen to you in spite of repeated requests, you may feel powerless.

Here's what helps me stay calm in such situations:

My boundary is my boundary. Period.

Once I know that I have a set a certain boundary, I don't need to move (for instance, playtime is playtime, bedtime is bedtime, etc.).

When you make a decision to stay firm on your boundaries, you are going to feel less of an energy drain.

This will also leave you with a lot of free time and energy to be able to take care of other household chores.

You can validate your child's experience or emotions in your own way, but yelling or getting upset when they cross your boundaries is only going to leave you feeling exhausted.

So, avoid this at all costs. You may need a few days to weeks to master this technique, but it's worth the effort.

Offer Choices and Alternatives

You can't discipline your kids without offering them choices.

If your child seems upset because of the boundary you set, he or she is not going to want to know about what they can or cannot do.

Look at it this way, as adults; do we like it when someone tells us that we don't have any choice?

No, right?

Then why would we want our toddler to like it?

Instead, start offering alternatives that the child can use to restore the balance of power.

When your child gets to choose between playing a game and eating his favorite porridge, he is more likely to make a better choice.

Always use these words when handling your toddler.

"You have two choices; either you brush your teeth right now, or have your milk.

Which one would you like?"

Believe me, disciplining your child is not child's play, but I promise you that it's not impossible either.

Using the right strategies without losing your mind is the key to getting your toddler to listen to you.

It's all about you showing and doing exactly what you need to.

Chapter Four: Common Parenting Mistakes And How To Avoid Them

I keep reminding fellow parents that we all make mistakes.

At the same time, I encourage them give themselves a break when they think they have made some mistakes.

It shouldn't be our goal to be perfect.

It takes time and patience for us to practice effective and positive parenting techniques.

I want all the parents to remember that your goal when dealing with your child's behavioral issues is not to be a perfect parent.

You just need to get back up after a slip-up and keep re-iterating good behavior.

Here are the top 5 common mistakes that most parents make.

Personalizing Their Child's Behavior

It can be a struggle not to take things personally especially if your child is behaving extremely rudely towards you.

You may assume that your toddler doesn't love you, or doesn't care about feelings.

But the truth is that he may not realize what he is doing.

After all, it's a toddler.

Keep that in mind the next time you feel like blaming yourself for his or her bad behavior.

Keep bringing your focus back to changing the child's behavior instead of taking it to heart.

Also, try not to lecture your kids when they don't behave rationally.

Not only is that ineffective, but it also makes the child respect you less.

Doing Everything By The Book

Most parents start reading several books or take advice from fellow parents when their baby is born.

The problem is that they also get stuck with some bookish knowledge even when their kid reaches the toddler stage.

They end up driving themselves mad just because some trick in the book did not work for them.

The truth is that there isn't a single way to parent a child.

Each toddler is different.

What works for someone else might not work for your toddler.

Instead of following every book in the house, focus on providing your child with a nurturing, loving and a safe environment to grow up in.

That alone is enough for everything else to fall into place.

Being Overly Protective

As parents of a toddler, we sense danger in every little thing or at every turn.

Of course, we mean well, but the overprotectiveness can actually end up being more harmful to the child.

If you constantly worry about your child, he or she may learn to be afraid of everyone or everything around them.

If your toddler seems to be specifically animal-friendly and spots a dog in the park, don't stop him from petting it.

At the same time, take care that the animal is friendly too and is free of infections.

Similarly, if your kid wants to make friends with strangers or smiles at them, simply allow them to while being alert of the surroundings.

Not Leaving The House

This is a big one.

When my son was born, I just didn't want to get out of the house fearing that the baby would fall over or something like that.

While I agree that toddlers are notorious and there's every possibility that they might break something, or hurt themselves, you can always have someone babysit them, or monitor them through hidden cams while you are out.

It is equally important for the baby to bathe in some sunshine and enjoy a nice drive or a walk.

The point is – don't hole up inside the house.

It's extremely unhealthy for your mental wellbeing as well as your child's.

Not Accepting Help

Even though you consider yourself as an independent mom or dad, it's a mistake to turn away any help that is offered to you.

It could be exhausting to do everything all by yourself.

Instead of letting parenting overwhelm you, you need to take it easy and accept if someone tries to help you with the kid.

Do not deny yourself any chance at enjoyment; otherwise, it can get difficult to cope with the emotional roller coaster you may have to get by every day.

You really don't have to be a supermom or a super dad. Allow your loved ones to take some time out and help you.

It will only make you a better parent.

Chapter Five: How To Be A Positive Role Model For Your Kid

Wondering how you can be someone who your child looks up to?

Well, here's a surprise.

You already are.

As I mentioned earlier, no parent is perfect, and perfection should not be your goal when parenting.

In fact, all parents are role models for their kids.

The only difference is the choices we make as to what kind of an ideal we want to set for our kids.

Do you want your kid to see you in a positive light?

Then you need to be a little mindful about how you act in front of them.

Kids are always watching us regardless of whether we are aware or not.

They keep storing our responses as a way to respond to situations in a similar manner.

Our kids are always watching and learning.

The key to being a positive role model for your child lies in your actions; they have a great influence on the way your kids grow up as adults.

We can preach to them as much as we like, but they are only going to follow our actions.

In order to actively become a role model for our toddlers, we need to start getting in tune with good behavior.

As parents, we should start looking inwards to learn how to manage all the stress that comes with being a parent.

I work with a lot of parents every day.

I often want to know about their favorite teachers, favorite mentors, or some peculiar behavior about their own parents that they find respectful.

Next, I ask them to share how this person reacted when they made a mistake.

Were they yelled at?

Beaten up?

Or shamed about it?

Not once have I got an answer in the affirmative.

Do you get my point?

The people we look up to are often the ones who treated us respectfully.

When we start holding ourselves accountable for setting up only positive behaviors we wish to see, then our children automatically do what we want them to do.

In fact, this way of getting things done from toddlers or anyone for that matter is the most effective.

What Exactly Do I Need To Do To Better Myself As A Parent?

Honestly, nothing, except for keeping your emotions in check and watching your behavior around your kid.

However, you may benefit from practicing meditation for about 20 minutes every day.

Here are a few things I learned through meditation which helped me become a positive role model for my son.

Be present

Meditation not only allows you to be present and become more mindful of your actions.

It's incredibly easy to forget to get your focus back on your actions.

But meditation can help you correct this habit.

For starters, if you meditate twice a day, then within a few days, you will start noticing how you are automatically able to focus on your actions effortlessly while dealing with your kid.

Remember the blue sky

Storm clouds can quickly start gathering in your mind, eventually affecting how we think.

That said, above all those clouds, is blue sky – a place where you can find contentment and peace.

There are days when I can't get anything right with my son and end up feeling like the worst parent in the world.

But when it's time to tuck my son into bed, I forget all my worries.

Don't forget to take a few minutes to fixate on the serene look on your kid's face while he or she is sleeping.

This will keep reminding you that all your efforts are worth it.

Be easy on yourself

When you are easy on yourself, you will be easy on your kid.

It's as simple as that!

There is no right or wrong way even when you try to meditate.

Just sit in silence for 5 minutes and allow all the thoughts to flow through you.

You should apply the same technique while trying to be a positive role model for your kid.

Also, you don't have to act positively all the time.

Go easy on yourself and don't beat yourself up if you accidentally happened to yell at your kid.

You can always apologize to your kid, and adjust your behavior later.

CPSIA information can be obtained
at www.ICGtesting.com
Printed in the USA
LVHW081214091019
633408LV00008B/2373/P

9 781798 520079